Dinosaur World
Tyrannosaurus Rex

by Lily Austen

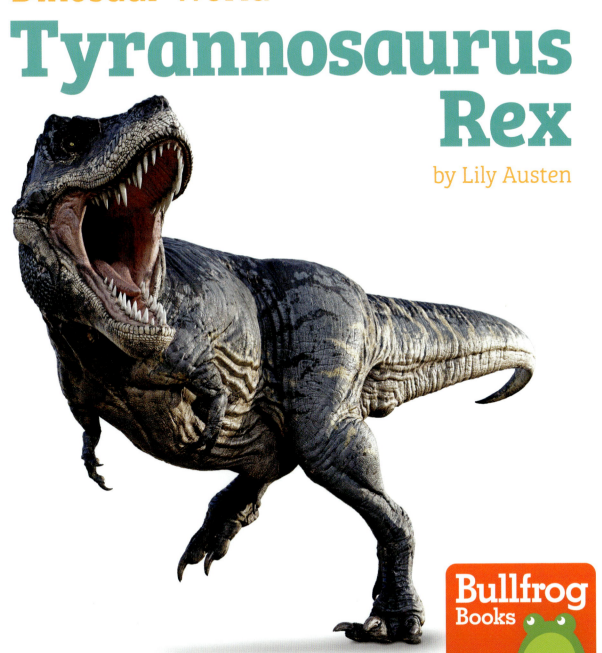

Bullfrog Books

Ideas for Parents and Teachers

Bullfrog Books let children practice reading informational text at the earliest reading levels. Repetition, familiar words, and photo labels support early readers.

Before Reading
- Discuss the cover photo. What does it tell them?
- Look at the picture glossary together. Read and discuss the words.

During Reading
- "Walk" through the book with the reader. Discuss new or unfamiliar words. Sound them out together.
- Look at the photos together. Point out the photo labels.

After Reading
- Prompt the child to think more. Ask: Tyrannosaurus rex is extinct. It no longer lives. It lived millions of years ago. What if you lived at the same time as a Tyrannosaurus rex?

Bullfrog Books are published by Jump!
3500 American Blvd W, Suite 150
Bloomington, MN 55431
www.jumplibrary.com

Copyright © 2026 Jump! International copyright reserved in all countries. No part of this book may be reproduced in any form without written permission from the publisher.

Jump! is a division of FlutterBee Education Group.

Library of Congress Cataloging-in-Publication Data

Names: Austen, Lily, author.
Title: Tyrannosaurus Rex / by Lily Austen.
Description: Minneapolis, MN: Jump!, Inc., [2026]
Series: Dinosaur world | Includes index.
Audience: Ages 5–8
Identifiers: LCCN 2024056702 (print)
LCCN 2024056703 (ebook)
ISBN 9798896620051 (hardcover)
ISBN 9798896620068 (paperback)
ISBN 9798896620075 (ebook)
Subjects: LCSH: Tyrannosaurus rex—Juvenile literature.
Classification: LCC QE862.S3 A97 2026 (print)
LCC QE862.S3 (ebook)
DDC 567.912/9—dc23/eng/20250115
LC record available at https://lccn.loc.gov/2024056702
LC ebook record available at https://lccn.loc.gov/2024056703

Editor: Alyssa Sorenson
Designer: Emma Almgren-Bersie

Photo Credits: Science Photo Library/Alamy, cover; Warpaint/Shutterstock, 1, 4, 8–9 (background), 12–13, 23bl (background); Herschel Hoffmeyer/Shutterstock, 3, 18–19 (background), 23tr (background); nonnie192/iStock, 5, 23br; Orla/Shutterstock, 6–7, 20–21; akiratrang/Adobe Stock, 8–9 (T. rex), 23bl (T. rex); IanGoodPhotography/iStock, 10; Warpaintcobra/iStock, 11, 23tl; Orla/iStock, 14–15; allvision/Adobe Stock, 16; Mohamad Haghani/Stocktrek Images/Science Source, 17; DM7/Adobe Stock, 18–19 (foreground), 23tr (foreground); freestyle images/Shutterstock, 22; 1 2 3D illustration/Shutterstock, 24.

Printed in the United States of America at Corporate Graphics in North Mankato, Minnesota.

Table of Contents

Strong Hunter	4
Parts of a Tyrannosaurus Rex	22
Picture Glossary	23
Index	24
To Learn More	24

**Tyrannosaurus rex
(tr-an-uh-SAW-ruhs REKS)**

Strong Hunter

Look! A Tyrannosaurus rex.

We call it a T. rex.

It **hunts** in a forest.
It **sniffs** the air.

It smells other dinosaurs.

They are close.

It watches.

It waits.

A dinosaur walks by.

**triceratops
(try-SEH-ruh-tops)**

The T. rex has long teeth.
They are sharp.

ROAR!

Another T. rex comes!

It is hungry, too.

They fight.

They bite each other.
Chomp!

One runs away.

Its tail is long.

It helps the T. rex **balance**.

tail

It looks for more food.

Parts of a Tyrannosaurus Rex

"Tyrannosaurus rex" means lizard king. T. rex was a powerful hunter. Take a look at the parts of a T. rex!

Picture Glossary

attacks
Uses violence against something.

balance
To stay steady and upright.

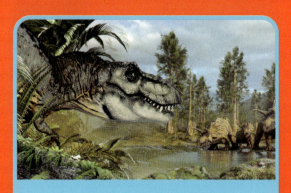

hunts
Looks for food.

sniffs
Smells.

Index

attacks 11
balance 18
bite 17
fight 16
food 21
forest 5
hungry 14
hunts 5
runs 18
sniffs 5
tail 18
teeth 13

To Learn More

Finding more information is as easy as 1, 2, 3.

❶ Go to **www.factsurfer.com**
❷ Enter **"Tyrannosaurusrex"** into the search box.
❸ Choose your book to see a list of websites.